Keto Diet Cookbook For Beginners #2019

Simple, Easy and Delicious Recipes for Busy People on Ketogenic Diet with 3-Week Meal Plan (Lose Up to 20 Pounds In 21 Days)

Amanda Whitley

Legal & Disclaimer

The information and contents herein are not designed to replace or take the place of any form of medical or professional advice and are not meant to replace the need for independent medical, financial, legal or other professional advice or services, as may be required. The content and information in this book have been provided for educational and entertainment purposes only.

The content and information in this book have been compiled from reliable sources and are accurate to the author's best knowledge, information, and belief. The author cannot guarantee this book's accuracy and validity and cannot be held liable for any errors and/or omissions. Further, changes will be periodically made to this book when needed. It is recommended that you consult with a health professional who is familiar with your personal medical history before using any of the suggested remedies, techniques, or information in this book.

Upon using the contents in this book, you agree to hold harmless the author from and against any damages, costs, and expenses, including any legal fees potentially resulting from the application of the information provided You agree to accept all risks associated with using the information presented inside this book.

Table of Content

Introduction

Greetings!! Thanks for getting this book, "The Ketogenic Diet For Beginners."

If you are considering the ketogenic diet or have started it and need a little help, this is the book for you. Maybe you aren't sure what's going on in your body or you're curious about what brands are keto-friendly. This book will clear all those questions up.

I love cooking, food, and I'm a keto dieter. I'm not a professional chef, doctor, or a nutritionist, but I've spent many hours researching the keto diet and cooking recipes. I'm no expert, but I would say I understand the diet more than most people. In this book, I've collected the most essential information and written it in a simple, easy-to-understand way. The keto diet can get confusing, especially once you get into the science side, but I hope I've had distilled everything in a way that's easy to grasp.

On the keto diet, you can eat food like delicious grass-fed steaks, full-fat butter, and baked goods sweetened with stevia. Sound like a diet you could get behind? Keep reading and let's learn more!

Chapter 1: The History and Science of the Ketogenic Diet

Before we get into the specific foods you can and can't eat on the ketogenic diet and how to succeed, it's good to know where the diet came from and how it works on a scientific level. The keto diet has origins stretching back to ancient times, but it took a thousand years before scientists knew exactly what was going on.

A prescription for seizures

People have suffered from seizures and epilepsy for thousands of years. Back in ancient Greece and India, the most common treatment was to stop eating or drinking. For some reason, fasting seemed to be prevent whatever was causing the seizures. For centuries, that was what patients had to go through - fasting or seizures. In 1911, French doctors developed a diet that could relieve seizures. It was vegetarian and low in calories. A few decades later, another doctor began experimenting, and learned that a diet low in carbs and high in fat also prevented seizures. Why?

Ketones are the key

When you fast, your body begins producing compounds known as "ketones." These are distributed through the body as fuel, because the body needs *something* to continue functioning normally. These compounds also show up when you restrict your carb intake, because the body normally depends on carbs for energy. When you replace most of your carbs with fat, the body begins to turn fatty acids into ketones, and depends on those for fuel instead. Unlike carbs, however, excess ketones are not stored as body fat.

That doesn't mean you should stop eating carbs completely. That's actually very unhealthy, if not impossible. You can eat significantly less, however, and choose the quality of carbs. Refined carbs like sugar and white bread don't offer much nutrition, so they mostly end up as body fat. Complex carbs like vegetables and fruit are much higher in good minerals and vitamins, so the carbs you do eat on the ketogenic diet are always complex. Less carbs trigger ketosis, which is the name of the ketone-producing process. That is what prevents seizures and results in other benefits, which we'll discuss a bit later on.

The magic percentage

Ketosis begins when your daily diet consists of a certain percentage of carbs, fat, and protein. That percentage is a mere 5-10% carbs, 15-30% protein, and 60-75% fat. For most people, that means eating just 20 grams of net carbs per day. For the record, a single slice of white bread has 13 grams. If you want to stay in ketosis, most meals should have just 7 net carbs per serving. What's the difference between net carbs and total carbs? Total carbs count fiber, while net carbs doesn't. That's why complex carbs like vegetables are a much better choice, because even though they may have a fairly large amount of carbs, they also have a lot more fiber than, say, white bread or candy.

What's the MCT diet?

In your exploration of the ketogenic diet, you might have seen the abbreviation "MCT" pop up. That stands for medium-chain triglycerides, which is the hot fat for the ketogenic diet. It's found mostly in coconut products - especially coconut oil - and in smaller amounts in cheese and butter. This fat has been shown to promote a lot of ketone production, so lots of people eager to get into ketosis will focus on getting as much of it as possible. The MCT diet adjusts the percentage a little, so you're getting 30-50% of your total daily calories from MCT oils. Because MCT is more effective at producing ketones, you can have more carbs and protein while staying in ketosis. This makes the diet easier for a lot of people. The MCT diet was created in the 1970's, but it's more popular in the United Kingdom than the US.

How do you know when you're in ketosis?

Your body doesn't suddenly change once you're in ketosis. You actually have to measure your ketone levels by analyzing your urine, blood, or breath. To start getting benefits from the keto diet, you want levels to be around 0.5 mmol/L, which stands for millimoles per liter. Urine strips are most effective when you're just starting on the diet, because once you've been in ketosis for a while, the levels will actually go down. That's because your body has adjusted to actually using the ketone for fuel and not getting rid of it through your pee. A blood meter measures beta-hydroxybutyrate (BHB), and it's usually more accurate than a urine strip. If you want a simpler test, a breath analyzer gives you a good idea of both your BHB and acetone levels.

Reasons to try the ketogenic diet

The keto diet has stayed popular for years, and it's because of the many benefits dieter's report. Here are the top reasons to consider a low-carb diet:

The diet might make it easier to lose weight

When you cut out the highest-carb food from your diet, which includes sugar, you might experience weight loss. Combined with exercise, lots of people find they are finally able to reach their weight goals when on the ketogenic diet. This is because it isn't eating fat that makes people overweight; it's sugar and foods low in nutrients, but high in carbs. By eating less carbs and more nutrients, losing weight can become much easier.

The diet can provide a boost of energy

When you eat high-carb foods, your blood sugar rises quickly, and then crashes. Throughout the day, this rollercoaster of highs and lows is exhausting, and makes it hard to be productive. When you switch to high-fat foods and snacks, your energy levels become more staple. You'll have more consistent energy through all your activities. Your mental clarity can also improve, since the brain is mostly fat, and loves the fat found in keto staples like salmon, avocados, nuts, and coconut oil.

You won't feel hungry on the keto diet

A lot of diets are characterized by hunger. You are supposed to eat less and you end up feeling hungry all the time. That isn't a problem on the keto diet. The body uses fat and quality proteins a lot more efficiently than refined carbs, which rush through the system and leave you feeling empty quickly after eating. You won't need to snack during the day as much after filling keto meals, and that can result in weight loss, too.

The diet can result in healthier skin and hair

The keto diet is so effective at treating dry hair and skin, there's even a term for it: the "keto glow." Lots of people find that after switching to a keto diet, their hair becomes sleeker, shinier, and healthier. Dry or acne-scarred skin is also hydrated by all the good fats, while even finger and toenails can become stronger and healthier-looking. In addition to encouraging more foods that help hair and skin, cutting out sugar and processed foods on the keto diet most likely plays a role in the glow, as well.

The diet may help protect against serious diseases

While more studies are needed to support this reason, there is research out there that suggests the ketogenic diet may protect people from certain diseases. Healthy fats lower bad cholesterol, a major cause of heart disease, while losing weight is also healthy for the heart. As for the brain, at least one study showed that being in ketosis improves a person's memory. When given MCT oil, Alzheimer's patients' brains produced more ketones.

Reasons to maybe not try the ketogenic diet

While the ketogenic diet remains very popular, lots of studies and expert opinions are also coming out against it. It may not be right for everybody and may not be the best choice for a long-term eating strategy. It's important to know the downsides of the diet before making a big change. Here are the top criticisms:

It puts people at risk for micronutrient deficiency

All restrictive diets make nutritionists nervous. This is because you are eliminating foods that are actually healthy (like whole grains) in order to achieve a certain goal. With the keto diet, any food that throws you out of ketosis is off the table, and that includes a lot of foods rich in nutrients. Keto dieters are at risk for lacking specific vitamins and minerals like fiber, vitamin D, sodium, and others. You can address this problem by being intentional about your food choices and even taking supplements, but the risk is definitely something to consider before choosing the keto diet.

It's a challenging diet

The keto diet is not going to end up on any list named "The Easiest Diets To Follow." Beginning the diet is difficult right out of the gate, as most people experience what's known as the "keto flu." Symptoms like nausea, headaches, and fatigue are common as the body learns to rely on fat instead of carbs for fuel. Once you're through that and in ketosis, you have to work to *stay* in ketosis by only eating certain foods and a certain quality of food, like grass-fed beef. That can get expensive and makes shopping tricky. Many people end up deciding it's just not worth it, at least for the long-term.

It's dangerous for diabetics

Low-carb diets are dangerous for diabetics. Why? Ketones make the blood more acidic, and diabetics are more vulnerable to ketoacidosis than others. If you're diabetic and on the ketogenic diet, you have to be very aware of what your ketone levels are and watch for any symptoms of ketoacidosis, like stomach pains and dehydration. If your levels hit 0.6 mmol/L, you're starting to enter ketoacidosis, and any higher will require medical attention. For this reason, most doctors will not recommend the keto diet for diabetics.

Chapter 2: What You Can Eat And What You Should Avoid

For being a restrictive diet, the list of foods you can eat is relatively extensive. All kinds of meat and seafood (ideally grass-fed, wild-caught, and organic) are allowed, while all full-fat dairy is also encouraged. You can eat lots of low-carb vegetables, as well, though you're more limited on fruit. A banana every now and then shouldn't throw you out of ketosis, however, but you should always be careful about what else you eat that day. Here's a fairly complete list of everything

Food to Eat

Meat/seafood:

Beef (ideally grass-fed)

Eggs (ideally cage-free and organic)

Fish/shellfish (ideally wild-caught)

Goat

Lamb

Organ meats

Pork (ideally free-range and organic)

Poultry (organic)

Vegetables/fruit:

Alfalfa sprouts

Avocado

Berries (blackberries, raspberries, cranberries, etc)

Bell peppers

Bok choy

Broccoli

Button mushrooms

Cabbage	Onions
Cauliflower	Parsley
Celery	Radishes
Citrus (lemons, oranges, limes)	Sea vegetables
Cucumber	Spinach
Eggplant	Swiss chard
Garlic	Tomatoes
Kale	Watercress
Lettuce	Zucchini

Nuts/seeds (in moderation):

Almonds	Pecans
Brazil nuts	Pumpkin seeds
Chia seeds	Shredded coconut (unsweetened)
Flax seeds	Sunflower seeds
Macadamia nuts	Walnuts

Full-fat dairy:

Cheese (cheddar, parmesan, mozzarella, brie, ricotta, etc)

Cottage cheese

Cream cheese

Dairy-free milk alternatives (unsweetened almond milk, coconut milk, macadamia nut milk)

Greek yogurt (plain and unsweetened)

Heavy cream

Fats/oils:

Almond oil

Avocado oil

Cocoa butter

Coconut oil/coconut cream

Duck fat

Ghee (clarified butter)

Nut butters (in moderation)

Olive oil (cold-pressed extra-virgin)

Beverages:

Sparkling water + seltzers (w/out added sweeteners)

Unsweetened coconut water

Unsweetened coffee (or sweetened with natural o-calorie sweetener)

Unsweetened herbal tea (or sweetened with natural o-calorie sweetener)

Water

Baking/cooking supplies:

Almond flour

Baking powder/baking soda (aluminum-free)

Coconut aminos (soy sauce substitute)

Coconut flour

Erythritol/stevia blends

Fish sauce

Mayonnaise (w/out added sugar)

Monk fruit extract or powder

Psyllium husk (a thickener)

Spices + herbs

Sugar-free ketchup

Sugar-free yellow mustard

Vinegar (white, wine, and apple cider)

Xanthan gum (in very small amounts)

Foods to avoid

Knowing what to avoid on the ketogenic diet is determined by asking yourself two questions: Is it low-carb? Does it have artificial ingredients? Foods too high in carbs will throw you out of ketosis when you eat too much, while anything with artificial or processed ingredients also tends be too high in carbs, while also being just unhealthy. Here's what to avoid:

Processed meats:

Deli meat

Grain-fed meats

Hot dogs

Sausages

Grain:

Barley	Quinoa
Buckwheat	Rice
Corn	Wheat
Oatmeal	Wheat gluten

High-carb veggies and fruit:

Artichokes	Mangos
Bananas	Pears
Carrots	Pineapple
Clementines	Potatoes
Dried fruit	Squash
Fruit syrups	Sweet potatoes
Grapes	Watermelon
Jam/jelly	Yams
Kiwi	

Low-fat or fat-free dairy:

Fake butter alternatives	Low-fat/fat-free sour cream
Low-fat/fat-free cream cheese	Low-fat/fat-free yogurt

Skim milk

Beans/legumes:

Black

Chickpeas

Fava

Kidney

Lentils

Peas

White

Certain oils:

Canola

Corn

Grapeseed

Peanut

Sesame

Soybean

Sunflower

Refined + artificial sweeteners:

Agave

Aspartame

Cane sugar

Coconut sugar

Corn syrup

Equal

Honey

Maple syrup

Raw sugar

Saccharin

Splenda

Sucralose

White sugar

Other:

Alcohol

Baked goods + treats

Diet foods

Fast food

Chapter 3: How To Shop

When you change your diet significantly, grocery shopping can be stressful and confusing. That's why it's a really good idea to plan your meals beforehand and write down all the ingredients, so you know exactly what to get. As for foods with labels, what should you look for? Be on watch for alternative names for "sugar," "wheat," and bad oils and fats. Some are obvious, like date sugar or cornmeal, but others have much more chemical names. There are dozens of them, and if you ignore them, it can make getting and staying in ketosis difficult. If a food has one of these listed ingredients, skip it:

Arrowroot

Dextrin

Diglycerides

Glucitol

HFCS

Interesterified oils

Lactose

Lentil

Malt

Maltodextrin

Maltose

Manioc

Muscovado

Panocha

Safflower

Sago

Scant

Seitan

Shortening

Sucrase

Vegetable starch

Keto-approved brands

It would take forever to read through all the labels in a grocery store, so what are some brands that almost always use simple, keto-friendly ingredients? Here are some staples you can rely on:

Artisana Organics

This brand makes a wide variety of nut and coconut butters, spreads, and snacks. On their website, they even have a section dedicated to keto and paleo, so you can go right to that page for a set of essentials like coconut butter and almond butter. They also sell more unusual nut butters like pecan, walnut, and cashew.

Bob's Red Mill

This famous brand has all your baking essentials, like coconut flour, almond flour, psyllium husk, and shredded coconut. You can find them on Amazon or most grocery stores.

Organic Valley

For full-fat dairy, Organic Valley is a great option. Check out their Grassmilk line, which includes half-and-half, yogurt, and cheddar cheese produced by grass-fed cows. All their other products are from pasture-raised cows, so you can feel good about ricotta, mozzarella, and anything else from them, too.

Nick's Sticks

These meat sticks and jerky products are made from 100% grass-fed beef or free-range turkeys, and free from additives like hormones, nitrate, and so on. Flavors include traditional or spicy, which is made with jalapeno and other natural seasonings. You can see a full ingredient list right on a product's page.

Now Foods

This company has a dedicated section to their keto-friendly offerings, which include supplements and cooking supplies like raw almond flour, flavored stevia sweeteners, bone broth, nuts, and more. Their website has a thorough breakdown of all the tests their products go through, their stance on GMOs (they're committed to natural), and a list of ingredients they will not use.

US Wellness Meats

For grass-fed beef, organic chicken, pork, dairy, and even lamb and bison, US Wellness Meats is the place to go. They even have a keto tag on their website, so you can browse products specifically selected for their high fat content. The company also sells a variety of sauces and seasonings under the Primal Palate name, which are certified organic.

Wild Planet

For your seafood and chicken needs, Wild Planet has a wide range of quality canned products. The seafood industry in particular is plagued by sustainability issues, so getting your fish from Wild Planet is a great way to fight back.

A sample pantry list

What should you always have in your pantry? It will vary household to household based on what you and your family enjoy, but this list should give you a good idea of the meats, produce, and dairy that should always be on hand.

Meat + seafood

Frozen fish fillets

Canned fish

Grass-fed ground beef

Nitrate-free bacon

Organic chicken thighs

Fats + Oils

Avocado oil

Cold-pressed extra-virgin olive oil

Dairy

Full-fat cheddar cheese

Grass-fed butter

Heavy cream

Parmesan cheese

Plain, whole-milk Greek yogurt

Unsweetened coconut milk

Vegetables + fruit

Avocados

Bell peppers

Celery

Cucumbers

Garlic

Kale

Lemons

Lettuce

Onions

Raspberries (fresh or frozen)

Strawberries (fresh or frozen)

Tomatoes

Nuts + seeds

Sunflower seeds

Unsweetened almond butter

Whole almonds

Beverages

Ground coffee

Herbal tea

Sparkling water

Baking/cooking supplies

Almond flour

Aluminum-free baking powder

Beef bone broth

Coconut flour

Psyllium husk

Pure vanilla extract (sugar-free)

Stevia + erythritol blend

Sugar-free ketchup

Sugar-free yellow mustard

Sukrin Gold (brown sugar substitute)

Unsweetened dark cocoa powder

Chapter 4: How To Eat Out and Travel On The Keto Diet

When you're making food at home, you have total control about what goes into a meal. However, there will be lots of times when you don't want to cook at home. Can you go out to restaurants on the ketogenic diet? And what about when you're traveling? It is more than possible to stay faithful to your diet when you're away from your own kitchen. It just takes a little preparation.

How to eat at restaurants

You're going out to eat for a meal for whatever reason (a birthday celebration, hanging out with a friend, a date night, etc), but you know you need to stick to certain foods to stay in ketosis. Here's what to do to make sure that happens:

Look at the menu beforehand

The last thing you want to happen when you're going out is getting to a place and realizing there's nothing on the menu that's keto-friendly. The solution is to pick a restaurant beforehand and check out the menu. You can even call ahead and ask if the chef will let you substitute sides (like salad instead of bread) and what kind of cooking oil they rely on. Don't feel self-conscious about the questions; you're doing this for your health. Once you find a restaurant with keto options, you can keep going back without needing to go through the whole process again.

Remember the big three foods you can always have (and the three foods to avoid)

It can be overwhelming to look at a menu and try to figure out if everything is keto-friendly. When in doubt, remember that three major groups are always acceptable: meat, dairy, and vegetables. Pretty much every restaurant will have multiple dishes that meet this criteria. On the other side, remember the three foods you can't have: grain, beans, and sugar, which includes most fruit, salad dressings, anything artificial. You can pretty easily eliminate those ingredients from a meal, so it's based on meat, dairy, and veggies. That might mean getting a burger without the bun, a salad dressed with just olive oil instead of salad dressing, or a steak dinner with broccoli substituted for the usual mashed potatoes.

Know what alcoholic drinks are low-carb

If everybody is ordering drinks at your gathering, you don't have to resign yourself to just sparkling water. There are quite a few low-carb alcohol options that won't mess up ketosis. Dry red and white wines (including champagne) only have about 2 total carbs per glass, while hard, pure liquors like whiskey, vodka, gin, brandy, and even tequila have zero carbs. Just make sure you aren't adding anything to those spirits, like juice or tonic, since that will cause the carb content to skyrocket.

Have a game plan for dessert

Dinner is over and people are ordering dessert. You might be really tempted, so to participate in this part of the meal without cheating, order a cup of coffee. Add some cream or even butter to make the drink even more keto-friendly. If coffee isn't your thing, herbal tea is also fine. If the restaurant is offering it, consider getting something like a cheese plate if you want something to munch on. If you have a sweet tooth, look up restaurants that make keto-friendly desserts. It's becoming more easier to find these places since the keto diet is becoming so popular.

Your usual food routine can get really disrupted when you travel. Whether it's a road trip and stopping at a fast food joint, or going out to eat all the time on a vacation, traveling can be rough on your diet. Here's how to stay in ketosis:

Pack keto-friendly snacks

When you're traveling, whether it's by car or plane, always bring your own snacks. You never know when delays or other distractions might occur, and you find yourself hungry without many choices around you. By packing food beforehand, you'll always have a snack at the ready. Think keto-friendly protein bars, homemade fat bombs, nuts, meat sticks, cut veggies, coconut water, and so on. These are easy to carry in a suitcase or cooler (if you're driving), and full of nourishing, energy-boosting fat and protein.

If you're staying overnight (or longer) somewhere, get a place with a kitchenette

The closer you can stick to your normal meal routine, the better. If you're staying somewhere for a while, it's best to get a place where you can cook. Some hotels have basic kitchenettes, though if you want a more homey setting, AirBnB is ideal, and often lets you pay less than you would for a hotel. Check out the grocery stores and markets where you'll be and stock up on your favorite keto ingredients.

Live a little

The keto diet is challenging. When you're on vacation, you might want to relax a little and let loose. Maybe there's a really amazing dessert on the menu and you know it will be worth it. You can plan for these moments, so the keto diet isn't so rigid that it's affecting how much you enjoy your vacation. Anticipate wanting a carb-heavy treat or meal and plan some physical activities for that day. This lets you make room in your daily calorie percentages for that "cheat food."

Chapter 5: The Most Common Mistakes People Make On The Keto Diet

The ketogenic diet isn't the easiest to follow. You have to be careful to eliminate certain foods and ingredients like wheat and sugar, which like to hide in sometimes surprising foods, and you have to stick to your percentages of fat, protein, and carbs. People don't even think about certain things when they start out, which can make the diet harder or not as beneficial. Here are the most common mistakes to avoid (and what to do instead):

Mistake #1: Not planning ahead

You decide to go on the ketogenic diet and dive right in. Unfortunately, you still have a kitchen full of foods not allowed on the keto diet and no idea what to make for meals. You also don't know what restaurants have keto-friendly options or what brands you should look for at the store. This makes your new diet very difficult, and you always feel at a loss and tempted to break the diet. As soon as you make the decision to go keto, get rid of everything in your house that isn't keto-approved. Look up recipes and start meal-planning, so you know exactly what to get at the store. You'll feel much more prepared and less overwhelmed.

Mistake #2: Not anticipating the keto flu

The keto flu is what happens when your body transitions from burning carbs to burning fat. Symptoms include headaches, fatigue, and nausea. While most people get through it without too much trouble in a week or two, it can be uncomfortable, especially if you aren't prepared for it. If you go about your normal routine and don't know what to do when symptoms hit, you may start regretting your choice to go keto and back out. You'll feel discouraged and disappointed in yourself. If you accept that the keto flu is coming, however, you can do things to make it easier. Staying hydrated is very important, since you lose more water during this phase of the diet. You should also eat as much protein and fats as you need, without worrying about the percentages, and be sure to replenish your electrolytes (especially sodium) by drinking chicken broth with salt. If your symptoms are especially bad, it's okay to eat some clean carbs (like a sweet potato or high-carb fruit) to make the adjustment easier.

Mistake #3: Not adjusting your exercise routine

Some people worry that they can't build muscle on the keto diet, but you definitely can. You just have to adjust your routines and possibly the diet slightly to make the most of your workouts. Anaerobic exercise, which is intense and interval-based, isn't improved by the keto diet because it relies on carbs. You can still do this type of exercise, but you should eat 15-30 fast-acting carbs before and after a workout. Aerobic and cardio exercise, however, can improve with the keto diet and doesn't require any adjustments to your carb intake.

Mistake #4: Ignoring your electrolytes

Electrolytes are necessary to good health. On the keto diet, you lose them more than on other diets, especially during the first weeks of ketosis. Many people neglect these minerals, which can lead to potentially serious health problems. Be sure to get sodium, magnesium, potassium, and calcium through food or supplements, if necessary. Talk to your doctor about testing your levels, and be aware of how much you need per day for your best health.

Mistake #5: Not getting good sleep

Sleep is just as important to the body and mind as good food. Without good sleep, your health will suffer. A lot of people have terrible sleep habits, like getting distracted by their phone and computers in bed, never getting up at the same time, and so on. There's a lot you can do to improve your sleep quality. Make sure the room is completely dark and free from electronic blue lights, which have been shown to disrupt good sleep patterns. Start winding down an half or half-hour before bed, and turn off the TV and keep away from your phone and computer. Give your mind the chance to settle and prepare the body for sleep.

Mistake #6: Not finding support

When you change your diet dramatically, it will be hard. Lots of people believe they can do it alone, but they're soon overwhelmed and discouraged. It's very difficult to do anything by yourself; humans are built for community. To ensure long-term success, find a good support network, whether it's people who are going keto themselves, or are just really good listeners and cheerleaders. Consider looking online for a group on a website like MeetUp. You should also be clear with your family (if they aren't going keto with you) about what you need from them in terms of support. That might mean asking that they keep treats out of the house or that they agree to eating only keto meals if you're cooking. With good support, you'll find the motivation you need to stick to your diet.

Chapter 6 Quick and Easy Keto Recipes

Now that you've seen the three weekly meal plans you'll be following, it's time to take a look at the recipes! Remember, each of these recipes is made with just 6 main ingredients or less to ensure that they are quick and easy to prepare.

You'll notice that there are more recipes included here than are used in the meal plans. Consider them a bonus! Use these extra recipes to create meal plans of your own or swap out one of the recipes from the meal plans for something you prefer.

In the end, what really matters is that you stick to your macros so, however, you can get yourself to do it, call it a win!

Ham and Cheddar Omelet

Servings: 1

Ingredients:

- 3 large eggs
- 2 tablespoons heavy cream
- Salt and pepper
- 1 teaspoon olive oil
- ½ cup diced ham
- ¼ cup shredded cheddar cheese

Instructions:

1. Beat the eggs together with the heavy cream, salt, and pepper then set aside.
2. Heat the oil in a small skillet over medium-high heat.
3. Pour in the egg mixture and let it cook for 1 minute then lift the edges to spread the uncooked egg.
4. Keep cooking until the egg is almost set then sprinkle with cheese and ham.
5. Fold the omelet over then cook until the eggs are set.
6. Slide the omelet onto a plate and garnish with fresh chopped chives to serve.

Nutrition: 580 calories, 46g fat, 38g protein, 5g carbs, 1g fiber, 4g net carbs

Cream Cheese Pancakes

Servings: 3

Ingredients:

- ½ cup almond flour
- ½ (8-ounce) package cream cheese, softened
- 4 large eggs
- 1 tablespoon coconut oil or butter

Instructions:

1. Whisk together the almond flour, cream cheese, and eggs until smooth and well combined.
2. Heat the oil in a large skillet over medium heat.
3. Pour in the batter, using about 3 tablespoons per pancake.
4. Cook until bubbles form in the surface of the batter and the underside is browned.
5. Carefully flip the pancakes and cook until browned underneath.
6. Slide the pancakes onto a plate and repeat with the remaining batter.
7. Serve with sugar-free maple syrup, if desired.

Nutrition: 280 calories, 25g fat, 13g protein, 4g carbs, 1.5g fiber, 2.5g net carbs

Fried Eggs in Bell Peppers

Servings: 2

Ingredients:

- 1 teaspoon olive oil
- 1 medium red bell pepper, cored
- 6 large eggs
- Salt and pepper

Instructions:

1. Heat the oil in a large skillet over medium heat.
2. Slice the bell pepper into rings and place the rings in the skillet.
3. Fry for 2 minutes then flip the rings and crack an egg into the middle of each.
4. Season with salt and pepper then fry until the egg is done to your liking.

Nutrition: 255 calories, 17.5g fat, 19.5g protein, 6g carbs, 1g fiber, 5g net carbs

Bacon Egg Cups

Servings: 4

Ingredients:

- 12 slices uncooked bacon
- 10 large eggs
- ¼ cup sour cream
- ¾ teaspoon garlic powder
- ¼ teaspoon onion powder
- 1 cup shredded cheddar cheese

Instructions:

1. Preheat the oven to 375°F and grease a muffin pan with cooking spray.
2. Cook the bacon in a large skillet until slightly browned but still pliable then remove to paper towels to drain.
3. Whisk together the eggs, sour cream, garlic powder, and onion powder.
4. Stir in the cheese then season with salt and pepper.
5. Line each of the muffin cups with a slice of bacon then spoon in the egg mixture.
6. Bake for 20 minutes until the eggs are set then cool 5 minutes before serving.

Nutrition: 480 calories, 36.5g fat, 34g protein, 3g carbs, 0g fiber, 3g net carbs

Creamy Coconut Porridge

Servings: 1

Ingredients:

- ¼ cup canned coconut milk
- 1 tablespoon coconut oil
- 1 tablespoon coconut flour
- 1 large egg
- Pinch ground psyllium husk
- Pinch salt

Instructions:

1. Whisk together all of the ingredients in a small saucepan.
2. Cook over low heat, stirring constantly until it starts to steam.
3. Keep cooking until thickened to your liking then spoon into a bowl.
4. Top with heavy cream or coconut milk to serve.

Nutrition: 390 calories, 35g fat, 10g protein, 12g carbs, 6.5g fiber, 5.5g net carbs

Denver-Style Omelet

Servings: 1

Ingredients:

- 3 large eggs
- 2 tablespoons heavy cream
- Salt and pepper
- 1 teaspoon olive oil, divided
- ¼ cup diced yellow onion
- ¼ cup diced green pepper
- ¼ cup diced ham
- ¼ cup shredded cheddar cheese

Instructions:

1. Beat the eggs together with the heavy cream, salt, and pepper then set aside.
2. Heat ½ teaspoon of oil in a small skillet over medium-high heat.
3. Add the peppers and onions and sauté for 3 to 4 minutes until tender.
4. Spoon the veggies into a bowl and reheat the skillet with the remaining oil.
5. Pour in the egg mixture and let it cook for 1 minute then lift the edges to spread the uncooked egg.
6. Keep cooking until the egg is almost set then sprinkle half of it with the cooked veggies along with the ham and cheese.
7. Fold the omelet over then cook until the eggs are set.
8. Slide the omelet onto a plate and garnish with fresh chopped chives to serve.

Nutrition: 545 calories, 43g fat, 33g protein, 7.5g carbs, 1.5g fiber, 6g net carbs

Brussels Sprouts Hash

Servings: 4

Ingredients:

- 6 slices bacon, chopped coarsely
- 1 pound brussels sprouts, quartered
- 1 small yellow onion, chopped
- Salt and pepper
- 2 tablespoons water
- 4 large eggs

Instructions:

1. Cook the bacon in a large skillet until crisp then drain on paper towels.
2. Reheat the skillet with the bacon grease and add the brussels sprouts and onion, stirring to coat with bacon fat.
3. Cook for 4 to 5 minutes until the onions soften then season with salt and pepper.
4. Add the water then cover the skillet and steam the brussels sprouts until tender, about 5 minutes.
5. Spread the mixture evenly in the pan then make four depressions with a wooden spoon.
6. Crack an egg into each one then season with salt and pepper.
7. Cover and cook until the eggs are done to your liking then serve hot.

Nutrition: 205 calories, 11g fat, 15.5g protein, 12.5g carbs, 4.5g fiber, 8g net carbs

Cheesy Ham Egg Cups

Servings: 4

Ingredients:

- 12 slices smoked ham
- 1 cup shredded cheddar cheese
- 12 large eggs
- Salt and pepper

Instructions:

1. Preheat the oven to 375°F and grease a muffin pan with cooking spray.
2. Line each cup with a piece of ham.
3. Sprinkle in a little cheese then crack an egg into each cup.
4. Season with salt and pepper then bake 12 to 15 minutes until the eggs are cooked to your liking.

Nutrition: 465 calories, 31.5g fat, 40g protein, 5g carbs, 1g fiber, 4g net carbs

Bacon and Egg Roll-Ups

Servings: 6

Ingredients:

- 6 large eggs
- 2 tablespoons heavy cream
- Salt and pepper
- 1 tablespoon coconut oil
- 18 slices uncooked bacon
- 1 ½ cups shredded cheddar cheese

Instructions:

1. Whisk together the eggs, heavy cream, salt, and pepper.
2. Heat the coconut oil in a large skillet over medium heat then pour in the egg mixture.
3. Cook for 3 minutes, stirring often, until scrambled and done to your liking.
4. Lay out three pieces of bacon on a cutting board.
5. Sprinkle some of the cheese along the bottom third then add a spoonful of scrambled eggs.
6. Roll the bacon up around the filling and repeat with the remaining ingredients.
7. Reheat the skillet and add the roll-ups.
8. Cook for 1 to 2 minutes on each side until the bacon is crisp. Serve hot.

Nutrition: 375 calories, 30.5g fat, 24g protein, 1.5g carbs, 0g fiber, 1.5g net carbs

Three Cheese Omelet

Servings: 1

Ingredients:

- 3 large eggs
- 2 tablespoons heavy cream
- Salt and pepper
- 1 teaspoon olive oil
- 2 tablespoons shredded cheddar cheese
- 2 tablespoons shredded Swiss cheese
- 2 tablespoons grated parmesan cheese

Instructions:

1. Beat the eggs together with the heavy cream, salt, and pepper then set aside.
2. Heat the oil in a small skillet over medium-high heat.
3. Pour in the egg mixture and let it cook for 1 minute then lift the edges to spread the uncooked egg.
4. Keep cooking until the egg is almost set then sprinkle with the cheeses.
5. Fold the omelet over then cook until the eggs are set.
6. Slide the omelet onto a plate and garnish with fresh chopped chives to serve.

Nutrition: 615 calories, 48g fat, 39g protein, 3g carbs, 0g fiber, 3g net carbs

Eggs Baked in Avocado Boats

Servings: 2

Ingredients:

- 1 medium avocado
- 2 large eggs
- Salt and pepper
- 1 teaspoon fresh chopped chives

Instructions:

1. Preheat the oven to 350°F.
2. Cut the avocado in half and scoop some of the flesh out of each half.
3. Place the avocado halves in a baking dish and spray with cooking spray.
4. Crack an egg into each half and season with salt and pepper.
5. Bake for 20 minutes until the eggs are done to your liking then garnish with fresh chopped chives to serve.

Nutrition: 275 calories, 24.5g fat, 8g protein, 9g carbs, 7g fiber, 2g net carbs

Spinach Breakfast Bowl

Servings: 1

Ingredients:

- 2 slices bacon, chopped
- 3 cups fresh baby spinach
- Salt and pepper
- 1 tablespoon butter
- 2 large eggs

Instructions:

1. Cook the bacon in a large skillet over medium-high heat until crisp.
2. Drain the bacon on paper towel then reheat the skillet with the bacon grease.
3. Add the spinach then season with salt and pepper.
4. Cook for 2 to 3 minutes, stirring often, until wilted then place in a bowl.
5. Reheat the skillet with the butter and wait until it is hot.
6. Crack the eggs into the skillet and season with salt and pepper.
7. Cook until the eggs are done to your liking then serve over the spinach topped with crumbled bacon.

Nutrition: 370 calories, 30g fat, 22g protein, 4.5g carbs, 2g fiber, 2.5g net carbs

One-Pan Eggs and Peppers

Servings: 4

Ingredients:

- 10 large eggs
- 2 tablespoons heavy cream
- Salt and pepper
- 1 small red pepper, cored and chopped
- 1 small green pepper, cored and chopped

Instructions:

1. Preheat the oven to 350°F and grease a 9x13-inch glass baking dish.
2. Whisk the eggs and heavy cream in a bowl with the salt and pepper until frothy.
3. Add the peppers and stir well.
4. Pour the mixture into the baking sheet and spread it evenly.
5. Bake for 12 to 15 minutes until the egg is firm and cooked through.
6. Cool for 5 minutes then cut into pieces to serve.

Nutrition: 220 calories, 15g fat, 16g protein, 4.5g carbs, 1g fiber, 3.5g net carbs

Chocolate Protein Pancakes

Servings: 2

Ingredients:

- ½ cup canned coconut milk
- 2 tablespoons coconut oil
- 4 large eggs
- 1 scoop chocolate whey protein powder
- 2 tablespoons unsweetened cocoa powder
- Liquid stevia, to taste

Instructions:

1. Place the coconut milk, coconut oil, and eggs in a blender.
2. Pulse several times then add the protein powder and cocoa powder.
3. Blend the mixture until smooth then sweeten with liquid stevia to taste and blend smooth once more.
4. Heat a large nonstick skillet over medium heat.
5. Spoon the batter into the skillet, using about ¼ cup per pancake.
6. Cook until the underside of each pancake is browned then flip and cook until browned underneath.
7. Slide the pancakes onto a plate and repeat with the remaining batter.

Nutrition: 440 calories, 39g fat, 20g protein, 8g carbs, 3g fiber, 5g net carbs

Bacon Cheddar Chive Omelet

Servings: 1

Ingredients:

- 3 large eggs
- 2 tablespoons heavy cream
- Salt and pepper
- 2 slices bacon, chopped
- ¼ cup shredded cheddar cheese
- 1 tablespoon fresh chopped chives

Instructions:

1. Beat the eggs together with the heavy cream, salt, and pepper then set aside.
2. Cook the bacon in a small skillet over medium-high heat until crisp.
3. Spoon the bacon off into a bowl and reheat the skillet with the bacon grease.
4. Pour in the egg mixture and let it cook for 1 minute then lift the edges to spread the uncooked egg.
5. Keep cooking until the egg is almost set then sprinkle with the cooked bacon along with the cheddar cheese and chives.
6. Fold the omelet over then cook until the eggs are set.
7. Slide the omelet onto a plate and serve hot.

Nutrition: 535 calories, 43g fat, 34g protein, 3g carbs, 0g fiber, 3g net carbs

Balsamic Spinach Salad with Avocado

Servings: 3

Ingredients:

- ¼ cup olive oil
- 2 tablespoons balsamic vinegar
- 1 teaspoon Dijon mustard
- 5 cups fresh baby spinach
- 1 medium avocado, sliced thin

Instructions:

1. Whisk together the olive oil, balsamic vinegar, and Dijon mustard in a salad bowl.
2. Toss with the spinach then divide between two salad plates.
3. Top each salad with sliced avocado to serve.

Nutrition: 295 calories, 30g fat, 3g protein, 8g carbs, 6g fiber, 2g net carbs

Cheesy Cauliflower Soup

Servings: 3

Ingredients:

- 2 cups chicken broth
- 1 small head cauliflower, chopped
- 1 clove minced garlic
- ½ cup heavy cream
- ½ cup shredded cheddar cheese
- Salt and pepper

Instructions:

1. Warm the chicken broth in a medium saucepan over medium heat.
2. Add the cauliflower and garlic then bring to a boil.
3. Reduce heat and simmer for 15 minutes until the cauliflower is tender
4. Stir in the cream and cheese then season with salt and pepper.
5. Blend or use an immersion blender to puree and serve hot.

Nutrition: 195 calories, 15g fat, 10g protein, 6.5g carbs, 2g fiber, 4.5g net carbs

Chopped Salad with Tuna

Servings: 2

Ingredients:

- 3 cups fresh chopped romaine
- ½ cup cherry tomatoes, halved
- ½ cup chopped cucumber, seedless
- ¼ cup diced red onion
- 1 lemon, juiced
- 2 (5-ounce) cans tuna in water

Instructions:

1. Combine the romaine lettuce, tomatoes, cucumber, and red onion in a large salad bowl.
2. Toss with lemon juice then season with salt and pepper.
3. Divide the salad among two plates.
4. Drain and flake the tuna then divide it between the two salads to serve.

Nutrition: 205 calories, 4.5g fat, 34.5g protein, 5g carbs, 1g fiber, 4g net carbs

Pumpkin Ginger Soup

Servings: 3

Ingredients:

- 1 cup fresh pumpkin
- 1 tablespoon olive oil
- ½ small yellow onion, chopped
- 1 clove minced garlic
- 1 tablespoon grated ginger
- 2 cups chicken broth

Instructions:

1. Bring a pot of salted water to boil then add the fresh pumpkin.
2. Boil until the pumpkin is soften then drain and mash it well.
3. Heat the oil in a saucepan over medium heat.
4. Add the onion, garlic, and ginger then cook for 3 minutes, stirring.
5. Add the pumpkin then cook for 2 minutes.
6. Stir in the chicken broth then bring to a boil.
7. Reduce heat and simmer for 20 minutes then remove from heat.
8. Puree the soup using an immersion blender then adjust seasoning to taste.

Nutrition: 60 calories, 9g fat, 7g protein, 15g carbs, 5g fiber, 10g net carbs

Bacon Arugula Salad with Mushrooms

Servings: 2

Ingredients:

- 3 slices bacon
- 1 cup sliced mushrooms
- 1 small shallot, sliced thin
- 4 cups fresh baby arugula

Instructions:

1. Cook the bacon in a skillet until crisp then remove to paper towels to drain.
2. Spoon all but 1 tablespoon of bacon fat out of the skillet and reheat it.
3. Add the mushrooms and shallots then sauté until they are tender, about 4 to 6 minutes.
4. Divide the arugula between two salad bowls.
5. Top with the mushrooms and crumble the bacon over the salads.
6. Serve with olive oil and vinegar.

Nutrition: 105 calories, 6.5g fat, 8g protein, 4.5g carbs, 1g fiber, 3.5g net carbs

Broccoli Cheddar Soup

Servings: 4

Ingredients:

- 1 tablespoon butter
- ½ small white onion, diced
- 1 cup chopped broccoli
- 2 cups chicken broth
- ¼ cup heavy cream
- 1 cup shredded cheddar cheese

Instructions:

1. Sauté the onion in butter in a saucepan over medium heat until the onions are translucent.
2. Stir in the broccoli and chicken broth then bring to a boil.
3. Reduce heat and simmer until the broccoli is tender, about 10 to 12 minutes.
4. Stir in the cream then season with salt and pepper.
5. Remove from heat then stir in the cheddar cheese. Serve hot.

Nutrition: 200 calories, 16g fat, 10.5g protein, 3.5g carbs, 1g fiber, 2.5g net carbs

Tuna Salad on Lettuce

Servings: 3

Ingredients:

- 1 (5-ounce) can tuna in water, drained
- 1 medium stalk celery, diced
- ½ cup mayonnaise
- 1 tablespoon lemon juice
- 1 teaspoon Dijon mustard
- 3 cups chopped romaine lettuce

Instructions:

1. Flake the tuna into a bowl then add the celery.
2. Stir in the mayonnaise, lemon juice, and mustard then season with salt and pepper.
3. Serve the tuna salad over chopped lettuce.

Nutrition: 315 calories, 28g fat, 11.5g protein, 2.5g carbs, 1g fiber, 1.5g net carbs

Buffalo Chicken Soup

Servings: 4

Ingredients:

- 2 tablespoons butter
- ½ small yellow onion, chopped
- 2 cups half-n-half
- 1 cup chopped chicken breast
- 2 tablespoons hot sauce
- 1 cup shredded cheddar cheese

Instructions:

1. Heat the butter in a saucepan on medium-high heat.
2. Add the onion and sauté until tender then stir in the flour.
3. Cook for another 2 minutes then add the half-and-half.
4. Stir in the chicken, hot sauce, and cheddar cheese then season with salt and pepper.
5. Reduce heat and simmer on medium-low until the cheese is melted, about 10 minutes.

Nutrition: 355 calories, 30g fat, 16g protein, 6.5g carbs. 0.5g fiber, 6g net carbs

Spinach Salad with Bacon Dressing

Servings: 2

Ingredients:

- 4 cups fresh baby spinach
- 4 slices bacon
- 1 ½ tablespoons apple cider vinegar
- 2 teaspoons honey
- 2 teaspoon Dijon mustard
- 2 hard-boiled eggs, sliced

Instructions:

1. Divide the spinach between two salad plates.
2. Cook the bacon in a small skillet over medium-high heat until crisp.
3. Remove the bacon to paper towels to drain then crumble.
4. Spoon all but 2 tablespoons of bacon grease out of the skillet then reheat it.
5. Whisk in the vinegar, honey, and mustard then season with salt and pepper.
6. Cook until warmed then drizzle over the salads.
7. Top each salad with sliced egg to serve.

Nutrition: 210 calories, 13g fat, 14.5g protein, 9g carbs, 1.5g fiber, 7.5g net carbs

Cucumber Avocado Soup

Servings: 3

Ingredients:

- 1 medium seedless cucumber, peeled and chopped
- 1 small avocado, chopped
- ¼ cup fresh cilantro
- 2 tablespoons apple cider vinegar
- 1 clove minced garlic
- ¾ cup water

Instructions:

1. Combine the cucumber, avocado, cilantro, vinegar, and garlic in a blender and blend until smooth and well combined.
2. Add up to 1 cup of water, a little at a time, until thinned to the desired texture.
3. Season with salt and pepper then chill until ready to serve.

Nutrition: 150 calories, 13g fat, 2g protein, 7.5g carbs, 5g fiber, 2.5g net carbs

Easy Egg Salad on Lettuce

Servings: 4

Ingredients:

- 6 large eggs
- 1 medium avocado, chopped
- 1/3 cup mayonnaise
- 1 teaspoon Dijon mustard
- 1 teaspoon lemon juice
- 3 cups fresh chopped romaine

Instructions:

1. Hard-boil the eggs to your liking then rinse in cold water and peel.
2. Chop the eggs into a bowl then season with salt and pepper.
3. Mash the avocado then stir it into the egg with the mayonnaise, mustard, and lemon juice.
4. Serve the egg salad chilled on chopped romaine lettuce.

Nutrition: 350 calories, 32g fat, 10.5g protein, 5g carbs, 3.5g fiber, 1.5g net carbs

Mexican Chicken Soup

Servings: 2

Ingredients:

- ½ pound boneless chicken thighs
- ½ cup diced tomatoes
- ½ small yellow onion, chopped
- 2 cloves minced garlic
- 1 cup chicken broth
- ½ cup shredded cheddar cheese

Instructions:

1. Combine the chicken, tomatoes, onion, and garlic in a slow cooker.
2. Pour in the chicken broth then season with salt and pepper.
3. Cover and cook on high heat for 2 to 3 hours then shred the chicken.
4. Stir in the cheddar cheese and cook for another 20 minutes.
5. Serve hot topped with sour cream and diced avocado.

Nutrition: 400 calories, 27g fat, 30g protein, 5g carbs, 1g fiber, 4g net carbs

Greek-Style Salad with Feta

Servings: 2

Ingredients:

- 2 tablespoons olive oil
- 1 tablespoon red wine vinegar
- 3 cups chopped romaine lettuce
- ½ cup diced seedless cucumber, peeled
- ½ cup kalamata olives, sliced
- 1.5 ounces feta cheese, crumbled

Instructions:

1. Whisk together the olive oil and red wine vinegar in a salad bowl.
2. Toss in the lettuce, cucumber, and olives.
3. Divide the salad between two salad bowls and top with feta to serve.

Nutrition: 230 calories, 22g fat, 4g protein, 6.5g carbs, 2g fiber, 4.5g net carb

Creamy Tomato Bisque

Servings: 3

Ingredients:

- 1 teaspoon olive oil
- ½ small yellow onion, chopped
- 2 cloves minced garlic
- 2 cups chicken broth
- 1 (14-ounce) can crushed tomatoes
- ¼ cup heavy cream

Instructions:

1. Heat the oil in a saucepan over medium heat.
2. Add the onion and garlic then sauté until the onion is soft, about 6 minutes.
3. Stir in the chicken broth and tomatoes then bring to a simmer.
4. Cook for 30 minutes then remove from heat and blend smooth.
5. Stir in the heavy cream and season with salt and pepper.

Nutrition: 135 calories, 6g fat, 7g protein, 13g carbs, 4.5g fiber, 8.5g net carbs

Chopped Cobb Salad with Avocado

Servings: 2

Ingredients:

- 4 cups chopped romaine lettuce
- ½ medium avocado, diced
- 1 cup chopped chicken breast
- ½ cup cherry tomatoes
- 1 ounce blue cheese crumbles
- 2 hard-boiled eggs

Instructions:

1. Divide the romaine lettuce between two salad bowls.
2. Finely dice the avocado, chicken, and tomatoes.
3. Arrange the chopped ingredients on top of the two salads.
4. Sprinkle with blue cheese and top each salad with a hardboiled egg.
5. Serve with olive oil and vinegar.

Nutrition: 300 calories, 20g fat, 20.5g protein, 10.5g carbs, 4.5g fiber, 6g net carbs

Broccoli Salmon Casserole

Servings: 4

Ingredients:

- 1 tablespoon butter
- 1 pound fresh chopped broccoli
- 3 (6-ounce) cans Alaskan salmon, drained
- 1 cup heavy cream
- 1 tablespoon Dijon mustard
- 1 cup shredded cheddar cheese

Instructions:

1. Preheat the oven to 400°F and lightly grease an 8x8-inch glass dish.
2. Heat the butter in a medium skillet over medium heat then add the broccoli.
3. Sauté for 6 to 7 minutes until tender then spread in the baking dish.
4. Flake the salmon over the broccoli and season with salt and pepper.
5. Whisk the cream with the mustard and pour into the baking dish.
6. Sprinkle with cheddar cheese then bake for 20 minutes until hot and bubbling.

Nutrition: 495 calories, 33g fat, 41g protein, 9g carbs, 3g fiber, 6g net carbs

Steak and Pepper Kebabs

Servings: 3

Ingredients:

- 12 ounces sirloin steak
- 2 tablespoons olive oil
- 1 ½ tablespoons balsamic vinegar
- 1 teaspoon Dijon mustard
- Salt and pepper
- 2 small red peppers, cored and cut into chunks

Instructions:

1. Cut the beef into cubes and toss with olive oil, balsamic vinegar, and mustard.
2. Slice the beef onto metal skewers with the peppers.
3. Season the kebabs with salt and pepper.
4. Preheat the grill to high heat and grease the grates with oil.
5. Place the kebabs on the grill and cook for 2 to 3 minutes on each side until the steak is done to your liking.

Nutrition: 320 calories, 16.5g fat, 35g protein, 6g carbs, 1g fiber, 5g net carbs

Smothered Pork Chops

Servings: 3

Ingredients:

- 1 tablespoon olive oil
- 2 cups sliced mushrooms
- ½ small yellow onion, sliced thin
- 12 ounces boneless pork loin chops
- ¼ cup chicken broth
- ½ cup heavy cream

Instructions:

1. Heat the oil in a large skillet on medium-high heat.
2. Add the mushrooms and onions then sauté until browned, about 5 minutes.
3. Season the pork with salt and pepper then add to the skillet.
4. Cook for 3 minutes then turn the pork chops over and lower the heat to medium.
5. Cook for 8 to 10 minutes until the pork is cooked through then remove to a cutting board to rest.
6. Pour the broth into the skillet and simmer, scraping up the browned bits, until the liquid cooks off.
7. Stir in the cream and simmer until hot then spoon over the pork to serve.

Nutrition: 290 calories, 16g fat, 32g protein, 3.5g carbs, 1g fiber, 2.5g net carbs

Herb-Roasted Chicken

Servings: 4

Ingredients:

- 8 bone-in chicken thighs
- 1 tablespoon olive oil
- 2 cups chopped cauliflower
- 1 ½ cups sliced green beans
- ¼ cup chicken broth
- 1 tablespoon dried herbs (your choice)

Instructions:

1. Preheat the oven to 450°F and lightly grease a glass baking dish.
2. Heat the oil in a large skillet over medium-high heat.
3. Season the chicken with salt and pepper then add to the skillet.
4. Cook skin-side down for 3 to 4 minutes until the skin is browned then flip and cook for another 2 minutes on the other side.
5. Toss the veggies with the chicken broth and spread in the baking dish.
6. Place the chicken skin-side down on top of the veggies and roast 30 minutes.
7. Turn the chicken skin-side up and sprinkle with herbs.
8. Roast for another 25 to 30 minutes until cooked through then serve with the roasted veggies.

Nutrition: 420 calories, 29g fat, 32g protein, 6g carbs, 3g fiber, 3g net carbs

Grilled Pesto Salmon

Servings: 2

Ingredients:

- 2 (6-ounce) boneless salmon fillets
- Salt and pepper
- 16 spears asparagus
- 1 tablespoon olive oil
- 2 tablespoons pesto
- Lemon wedges

Instructions:

1. Preheat a grill pan to high heat and grease with cooking spray.
2. Season the salmon with salt and pepper then place it on the grill.
3. Toss the asparagus with the oil and place on the grill – cook until tender, turning occasionally as needed.
4. Cook the salmon for 4 to 5 minutes on each side until cooked to your liking.
5. Spread the pesto over the salmon and serve with lemon wedges.

Nutrition: 390 calories, 24g fat, 38.5g protein, 8.5g carbs, 4.5g fiber, 4g net carbs

Cheese-Stuffed Burgers

Servings: 3

Ingredients:

- 12 ounces ground beef (80% lean)
- 3 tablespoons almond flour
- 1 large egg
- ¾ cups shredded cheddar cheese
- 1 tablespoon olive oil
- 1 head Boston lettuce, leaves separated

Instructions:

1. Stir together the ground beef, almond flour, egg, and cheese in a bowl.
2. Season with salt and pepper then divide into 3 patties.
3. Heat the oil in a large skillet on medium-high heat then add the burgers.
4. Cook for 5 minutes then flip the burgers and cook to your liking.
5. Serve the burgers with your favorite keto burger toppings on lettuce leaves.

Nutrition: 400 calories, 23g fat, 44g protein, 2g carbs, 1g fiber, 1g net carbs

Rosemary Pork Tenderloin

Servings: 3

Ingredients:

- 1 ¼ pounds boneless pork tenderloin
- 1 tablespoon butter
- 1 tablespoon fresh chopped rosemary
- Salt and pepper
- 1 tablespoon olive oil
- 2 cups chopped broccoli

Instructions:

1. Rub the pork tenderloin with butter then season with rosemary, salt, and pepper.
2. Heat the oil in a large skillet over medium-high heat.
3. Place the pork in the hot skillet and cook for 2 to 3 minutes on each side to sear.
4. Add the broccoli to the skillet around the pork.
5. Reduce heat and cook on low, covered, for 8 to 10 minutes until the pork reaches an internal temperature of 145°F.

Nutrition: 300 calories, 14g fat, 37g protein, 6.5g carbs, 2g fiber, 4.5g net carbs

Seared Lamb Chops

Servings: 2

Ingredients:

- 4 bone-in lamb chops
- Salt and pepper
- 1 tablespoon olive oil
- 1 tablespoon butter
- 1 ½ cups sliced green beans

Instructions:

1. Season the lamb with salt and pepper.
2. Heat the oil in a large skillet over medium-high heat.
3. Add the lamb chops to the skillet and cook for 2 minutes until seared.
4. Turn the lamb chops and cook for 2 to 3 minutes on the other side until seared.
5. Remove the lamb chops to a cutting board to rest and reheat the skillet.
6. Melt the butter then add the green beans.
7. Sauté the green beans until tender then serve with the lamb chops.

Nutrition: 360 calories, 22g fat, 36g protein, 6g carbs, 3g fiber, 3g net carbs

Almond-Crusted Haddock

Servings: 4

Ingredients:

- 4 (6-ounce) boneless haddock fillets
- Salt and pepper
- ¼ cup almond flour
- 3 tablespoons chopped almonds
- ½ teaspoon garlic powder
- 1 large egg

Instructions:

1. Preheat the oven to 350°F and line a baking sheet with parchment.
2. Season the fish with salt and pepper.
3. Combine the almond flour, chopped almonds, and garlic powder in a shallow dish.
4. Whisk the egg then dip the fish fillets in the egg and dredge in the almond mixture.
5. Place the fillets on the baking sheet and bake for 12 to 15 minutes until the flesh flakes easily with a fork.
6. Serve the almond-crusted haddock with lemon wedges.

Nutrition: 230 calories, 8g fat, 35.5g protein, 2.5g carbs, 1g fiber, 1.5g net carbs

Curry Chicken and Broccoli

Servings: 4

Ingredients:

- ½ tablespoon curry powder
- 1 teaspoon garlic powder
- 1 teaspoon ground cumin
- 1 ½ pounds boneless chicken thighs
- 2 tablespoons olive oil
- 3 cups fresh chopped broccoli

Instructions:

1. Preheat the oven to 425°F and line a baking sheet with parchment.
2. Whisk together the curry powder, garlic powder, and cumin in a small bowl.
3. Toss the chicken thighs to coat with oil then sprinkle with the spice mixture and toss to coat it.
4. Place the chicken thighs on the baking sheet and add the broccoli around it.
5. Bake for 45 to 50 minutes until the chicken is done and the broccoli tender.

Nutrition: 450 calories, 33g fat, 32g protein, 6g carbs, 2.5g fiber, 3.5g net carbs

Pepper Grilled Steak

Servings: 4

Ingredients:

- 1 medium head cauliflower, chopped
- 2 tablespoons olive oil
- 1 pound ribeye steak
- Fresh ground pepper

Instructions:

1. Preheat the oven to 400°F and line a baking sheet with foil.
2. Toss the cauliflower with the oil and spread it on the baking sheet.
3. Season with salt and pepper, bake for 25 minutes while you prepare the steak.
4. Generously pepper the steak and season it with salt.
5. Grease an oven-proof skillet with cooking spray and heat it over high heat.
6. Add the steak and cook for 2 minutes then turn the steak over.
7. Transfer the steak to the oven and cook for 5 minutes or until done to your liking.
8. Serve the steak sliced with the roasted cauliflower.

Nutrition: 475 calories, 40g fat, 22g protein, 7.5g carbs, 3.5g fiber, 4g net carbs

Sesame Chicken Wings

Servings: 4

Ingredients:

- 3 tablespoons soy sauce
- 1 ½ tablespoons sesame oil
- 2 teaspoon balsamic vinegar
- 2 cloves minced garlic
- 16 chicken wing pieces
- 1 tablespoon sesame seeds

Instructions:

1. Whisk together the soy sauce, sesame oil, balsamic vinegar, and garlic.
2. Place the chicken wings in a zippered freezer bag and pour in the sauce.
3. Shake until well coated then marinate in the fridge for 2 hours.
4. Preheat the oven to 400°F and line a baking sheet with foil.
5. Remove the wings from the bag and shake off the extra sauce.
6. Place the wings on the baking sheet and bake for 35 minutes.
7. Sprinkle with sesame seeds and serve hot.

Nutrition: 460 calories, 33g fat, 38g protein, 2g carbs, 0.5g fiber, 1.5g net carbs

Cheesy Sausage Casserole

Servings: 6

Ingredients:

- 1 pound mild Italian ground sausage
- 8 ounces sliced mushrooms
- ½ small yellow onion, chopped
- 1 cup shredded cheddar jack cheese
- 8 large eggs
- ½ cup heavy cream

Instructions:

1. Preheat the oven to 375°F and grease a medium baking dish.
2. Cook the sausage in a skillet over medium-high heat until browned.
3. Stir in the mushrooms and onions and sauté until tender, about 6 to 8 minutes.
4. Spread the mixture in the baking dish and sprinkle with cheese.
5. Whisk together the eggs and heavy cream then pour over the ingredients.
6. Bake for 35 minutes until hot and bubbling.

Nutrition: 440 calories, 33g fat, 27g protein, 4.5g carbs, 1g fiber, 3.5g net carbs

Easy Shrimp Curry

Servings: 4

Ingredients:

- 2 cups chopped cauliflower
- 1 teaspoon olive oil
- 1 cup canned coconut milk
- 1 tablespoon minced garlic
- 1 teaspoon garam masala
- 1 pound large uncooked shrimp, peeled and deveined

Instructions:

1. Place the cauliflower in a food processor and pulse until it forms rice-like grains.
2. Heat the oil in a large skillet over medium heat.
3. Add the cauliflower and sauté for 6 to 8 minutes until tender.
4. Stir in the coconut milk, garlic, and garam masala then bring to a simmer.
5. Add the shrimp and simmer until they are just cooked through. Serve hot.

Nutrition: 225 calories, 16g fat, 17g protein, 6.5g carbs, 2.5g fiber, 4g net carbs

Turkey-Stuffed Peppers

Servings: 3

Ingredients:

- 1 small head cauliflower, chopped
- 1 teaspoon olive oil
- 12 ounces mild Italian ground sausage
- 1 teaspoon dried oregano
- 3 small bell peppers
- ½ cup shredded mozzarella cheese

Instructions:

1. Preheat the oven to 350°F.
2. Place the cauliflower in a food processor and pulse until it forms rice-like grains.
3. Heat the oil in a large skillet over medium heat.
4. Add the cauliflower and sauté for 6 to 8 minutes until tender.
5. Spoon the cauliflower rice into a bowl and reheat the skillet with the sausage.
6. Cook until the sausage is browned then stir the cauliflower back in.
7. Add the oregano then season with salt and pepper.
8. Slice the tops off the peppers and spoon the meat mixture into them then sprinkle with cheese.
9. Place the peppers in a dish and bake for 30 minutes, covered.
10. Uncover and bake for another 15 minutes until the peppers are tender.

Nutrition: 430 calories, 29g fat, 24g protein, 15g carbs, 4g fiber, 11g net carbs

Snacks and Smoothies

Almond Green Smoothie

Servings: 1

Ingredients:

- 1 cup unsweetened almond milk
- ½ cup full-fat Greek yogurt, plain
- 1 cup fresh baby spinach
- 1 small stalk celery, sliced
- ½ tablespoon almond butter
- Liquid stevia, to taste

Instructions:

1. Combine all of the ingredients in a blender.
2. Pulse several times then blend until smooth.
3. Sweeten to taste with liquid stevia then blend smooth.
4. Pour into a large glass and enjoy immediately.

Nutrition: 220 calories, 14g fat, 14g protein, 10.5g carbs, 3g fiber, 7.5g net carbs

Red Velvet Cake Smoothie

Servings: 1

Ingredients:

- 1 cup unsweetened almond milk
- ½ cup canned coconut milk
- ½ small beet, peeled and diced
- 1 teaspoon unsweetened cocoa powder
- ½ teaspoon vanilla extract

Instructions:

1. Combine all of the ingredients in a blender.
2. Pulse several times then blend until smooth.
3. Sweeten to taste with liquid stevia then blend smooth.
4. Pour into a large glass and enjoy immediately.

Nutrition: 295 calories, 28g fat, 4.5g protein, 11.5g carbs, 2.5g fiber, 9g net carbs

Avocado Spinach Smoothie

Servings: 1

Ingredients:

- 1 cup fresh baby spinach
- ½ cup diced avocado
- 1 cup unsweetened almond milk
- 4 to 5 ice cubes
- 1 tablespoon lemon juice
- Liquid stevia, to taste

Instructions:

1. Combine all of the ingredients in a blender.
2. Pulse several times then blend until smooth.
3. Sweeten to taste with liquid stevia then blend smooth.
4. Pour into a large glass and enjoy immediately.

Nutrition: 200 calories, 18g fat, 3.5g protein, 9.5g carbs, 6.5g fiber, 3g net carbs

Raspberry Coconut Smoothie

Servings: 1

Ingredients:

- 1 cup unsweetened almond milk
- ¼ cup canned coconut milk
- 4 fresh raspberries
- 4 to 5 ice cubes
- ½ teaspoon vanilla extract
- Liquid stevia, to taste

Instructions:

1. Combine all of the ingredients in a blender.
2. Pulse several times then blend until smooth.
3. Sweeten to taste with liquid stevia then blend smooth.
4. Pour into a large glass and enjoy immediately.

Nutrition: 220 calories, 18.5g fat, 3.5g protein, 14g carbs, 7g fiber, 7g net carbs

Almond Butter Protein Shake

Servings: 1

Ingredients:

- 1 cup unsweetened almond milk
- ¼ cup canned coconut milk
- 1 scoop vanilla whey protein powder
- ½ tablespoon almond butter
- Pinch ground cinnamon
- Liquid stevia, to taste

Instructions:

1. Combine all of the ingredients in a blender.
2. Pulse several times then blend until smooth.
3. Sweeten to taste with liquid stevia then blend smooth.
4. Pour into a large glass and enjoy immediately.

Nutrition: 345 calories, 24g fat, 26g protein, 9g carbs, 3.5g fiber, 5.5g net carbs

Cocoa Avocado Smoothie

Servings: 1

Ingredients:

- 1 cup unsweetened almond milk
- ½ cup chopped avocado
- 4 to 5 ice cubes
- 1 scoop chocolate whey protein powder
- Liquid stevia, to taste

Instructions:

1. Combine all of the ingredients in a blender.
2. Pulse several times then blend until smooth.
3. Sweeten to taste with liquid stevia then blend smooth.
4. Pour into a large glass and enjoy immediately.

Nutrition: 245 calories, 18.5g fat, 12.5g protein, 10g carbs, 6g fiber, 4g net carbs

Blueberry and Beet Smoothie

Servings: 1

Ingredients:

- 1 cup unsweetened almond milk
- ¼ cup canned coconut milk
- 1 tablespoon blueberries
- ½ small beet, peeled and chopped
- Liquid stevia, to taste

Instructions:

1. Combine all of the ingredients in a blender.
2. Pulse several times then blend until smooth.
3. Sweeten to taste with liquid stevia then blend smooth.
4. Pour into a large glass and enjoy immediately.

Nutrition: 205 calories, 18g fat, 3.5g protein, 11.5g carbs, 3.5g fiber, 8g net carbs

Choco-Macadamia Smoothie

Servings: 1

Ingredients:

- 1 cup unsweetened almond milk
- ¼ cup canned coconut milk
- 4 macadamia nuts, chopped
- 1 tablespoon unsweetened shredded coconut
- Pinch ground ginger
- Liquid stevia, to taste

Instructions:

1. Combine all of the ingredients in a blender.
2. Pulse several times then blend until smooth.
3. Sweeten to taste with liquid stevia then blend smooth.
4. Pour into a large glass and enjoy immediately.

Nutrition: 360 calories, 35g fat, 4g protein, 11g carbs, 5g fiber, 6g net carbs

Lemon Lime Smoothie

Servings: 1

Ingredients:

- 1 cup fresh chopped spinach
- ½ cup diced avocado
- 1 cup water
- 4 to 5 ice cubes
- 1 scoop vanilla whey protein powder
- 2 tablespoons fresh lemon juice
- 1 tablespoon fresh lime juice

Instructions:

1. Combine all of the ingredients in a blender.
2. Pulse several times then blend until smooth.
3. Sweeten to taste with liquid stevia then blend smooth.
4. Pour into a large glass and enjoy immediately.

Nutrition: 280 calories, 16.5g fat, 24.5g protein, 10g carbs, 5.5g fiber, 4.5g net carbs

Strawberry Cheesecake Smoothie

Servings: 1

Ingredients:

- 1 cup unsweetened almond milk
- 1 scoop vanilla whey protein powder
- 2 tablespoons cream cheese, softened
- ¼ cup fresh raspberries
- ½ teaspoon vanilla extract
- Liquid stevia, to taste

Instructions:

1. Combine all of the ingredients in a blender.
2. Pulse several times then blend until smooth.
3. Sweeten to taste with liquid stevia then blend smooth.
4. Pour into a large glass and enjoy immediately.

Nutrition: 325 calories, 21g fat, 26.5g protein, 9g carbs, 3g fiber, 6g net carbs

Pumpkin Pie Protein Shake

Servings: 1

Ingredients:

- 1 cup unsweetened almond milk
- ¼ cup canned coconut milk
- 1 scoop vanilla whey protein powder
- 2 tablespoons pumpkin puree
- ¼ teaspoon pumpkin pie spice
- Liquid stevia, to taste

Instructions:

1. Combine all of the ingredients in a blender.
2. Pulse several times then blend until smooth.
3. Sweeten to taste with liquid stevia then blend smooth.
4. Pour into a large glass and enjoy immediately.

Nutrition: 305 calories, 20g fat, 25g protein, 10g carbs, 3.5g fiber, 6.5g net carbs

Vanilla Chai Smoothie

Servings: 1

Ingredients:

- 1 cup unsweetened almond milk
- 1/3 cup canned coconut milk
- 4 to 5 ice cubes
- 1 teaspoon vanilla extract
- ¼ teaspoon ground cinnamon
- ¼ teaspoon ground ginger
- Pinch cloves

Instructions:

1. Combine all of the ingredients in a blender.
2. Pulse several times then blend until smooth.
3. Sweeten to taste with liquid stevia then blend smooth.
4. Pour into a large glass and enjoy immediately.

Nutrition: 265 calories, 25g fat, 3g protein, 8.5g carbs, 3.5g fiber, 5g net carbs

Lemon Avocado Smoothie

Servings: 1

Ingredients:

- 1 cup fresh baby spinach
- 1/2 cup chopped avocado
- 1 small stalk celery, chopped
- 1 cup cold water
- 4 to 5 ice cubes
- 1 tablespoon lemon juice

Instructions:

1. Combine all of the ingredients in a blender.
2. Pulse several times then blend until smooth.
3. Sweeten to taste with liquid stevia then blend smooth.
4. Pour into a large glass and enjoy immediately.

Nutrition: 160 calories, 14.5g fat, 2.5g protein, 8g carbs, 6g fiber, 2g net carbs

Cucumber Melon Smoothie

Servings: 1

Ingredients:

- 1 cup unsweetened almond milk
- ½ cup seedless cucumber, peeled and chopped
- ¼ cup chopped honeydew melon
- ¼ cup canned coconut milk
- 4 to 5 ice cubes
- 1 tablespoon lemon juice
- Liquid stevia, to taste

Instructions:

1. Combine all of the ingredients in a blender.
2. Pulse several times then blend until smooth.
3. Sweeten to taste with liquid stevia then blend smooth.
4. Pour into a large glass and enjoy immediately.

Nutrition: 205 calories, 18g fat, 3g protein, 11g carbs, 3g fiber, 8g net carbs

Cocoa Almond Smoothie

Servings: 1

Ingredients:

- 1 cup unsweetened almond milk
- ¼ cup canned coconut milk
- 1 scoop vanilla whey protein powder
- 1 tablespoon unsweetened cocoa powder
- Liquid stevia, to taste

Instructions:

1. Combine all of the ingredients in a blender.
2. Pulse several times then blend until smooth.
3. Sweeten to taste with liquid stevia then blend smooth.
4. Pour into a large glass and enjoy immediately.

Nutrition: 305 calories, 20.5g fat, 25.5g protein, 10g carbs, 4g fiber, 6g net carbs

Chocolate Almond Fat Bombs

Servings: 8

Ingredients:

- ½ cup coconut oil
- ½ cup almond butter
- ¼ cup cocoa powder
- 2 tablespoons coconut flour
- Liquid stevia, to taste
- 8 whole almonds

Instructions:

1. Combine the coconut oil and almond butter in a small saucepan over low heat until melted then whisk smooth.

2. Whisk in the cocoa powder along with the coconut flour.
3. Stir smooth then sweeten with liquid stevia to taste and remove from heat.
4. When the mixture hardens slightly, divide it into 8 pieces and roll into balls.
5. Top each ball with an almond then chill until firm.

Nutrition: 150 calories, 15.5g fat, 1.5g protein, 4g carbs, 2.5g fiber, 1.5g net carbs

Cashew Butter Fat Bombs

Servings: 8

Ingredients:

- ½ cup coconut oil
- ½ cup cashew butter
- ¼ cup unsweetened cocoa powder
- 2 tablespoons coconut flour
- Liquid stevia
- 8 whole cashews

Instructions:

1. Combine the coconut oil and cashew butter in a small saucepan over low heat until melted then whisk smooth.
2. Whisk in the cocoa powder along with the coconut flour.
3. Stir smooth then sweeten with liquid stevia to taste and remove from heat.
4. When the mixture hardens slightly, divide it into 8 pieces and roll into balls.
5. Top each ball with a cashew then chill until firm.

Nutrition: 240 calories, 23g fat, 4g protein, 8.5g carbs, 2.5g fiber, 6g net carbs

Macadamia Nut Fat Bombs

Servings: 8

Ingredients:

- ½ cup coconut oil
- ½ cup almond butter
- ¼ cup unsweetened cocoa powder
- 2 tablespoons coconut flour
- Liquid stevia
- 8 macadamia nuts

Instructions:

1. Combine the coconut oil and almond butter in a small saucepan over low heat until melted then whisk smooth.
2. Whisk in the cocoa powder along with the coconut flour.
3. Stir smooth then sweeten with liquid stevia to taste and remove from heat.
4. When the mixture hardens slightly, divide it into 8 pieces and roll into balls.
5. Top each ball with a macadamia nut then chill until firm.

Nutrition: 165 calories, 17g fat, 1.5g protein, 4g carbs, 2.5g fiber, 1.5g net carbs

Chocolate Sunflower Fat Bombs

Servings: 8

Ingredients:

- ½ cup coconut oil
- ½ cup sunflower seed butter
- ¼ cup unsweetened cocoa powder, divided
- 2 tablespoons coconut flour
- Liquid stevia, to taste

Instructions:

1. Combine the coconut oil and sunflower seed butter in a small saucepan over low heat until melted then whisk smooth.
2. Whisk in half the cocoa powder along with the coconut flour.
3. Stir smooth then sweeten with liquid stevia to taste and remove from heat.
4. When the mixture hardens slightly, divide it into 8 pieces and roll into balls.
5. Roll each ball in the remaining cocoa powder then chill until firm.

Nutrition: 230 calories, 22g fat, 4g protein, 8g carbs, 2g fiber, 6g net carbs

Sesame Seed Fat Bombs

Servings:

Ingredients:

- ½ cup coconut oil
- ½ cup almond butter
- ¼ cup unsweetened cocoa powder
- 2 tablespoons almond flour
- Liquid stevia
- ¼ cup toasted sesame seeds

Instructions:

1. Combine the coconut oil and almond butter in a small saucepan over low heat until melted then whisk smooth.
2. Whisk in the cocoa powder along with the almond flour.
3. Stir smooth then sweeten with liquid stevia to taste and remove from heat.
4. When the mixture hardens slightly, divide it into 8 pieces and roll into balls.
5. Roll each ball in the sesame seeds then chill until firm.

Nutrition: 165 calories, 17.5g fat, 2g protein, 3g carbs, 1.5g fiber, 1.5g net carbs

Classic Deviled Eggs

Servings: 12

Ingredients:

- 12 large eggs
- ½ cup mayonnaise
- 1 tablespoon Dijon mustard
- 2 teaspoons fresh lemon juice
- Salt to taste
- Paprika

Instructions:

1. Hard-boil the eggs then rinse in cool water and peel them.
2. Cut the eggs in half lengthwise and scoop the yolks into a bowl.
3. Mash the yolks with the mayonnaise, mustard, lemon juice, and salt.
4. Spoon or pipe the filling back into the eggs and sprinkle with paprika to serve.

Nutrition: 130 calories, 12g fat, 6.5g protein, 0.5g carbs, 0g fiber, 0.5g net carbs

Cinnamon Spiced Almonds

Servings: 4

Ingredients:

- 1 cup almonds, whole
- 1 tablespoon olive oil
- 1 teaspoon ground cinnamon
- Pinch salt

Instructions:

1. Preheat the oven to 300°F and line a baking sheet with foil.
2. Toss the almonds with the olive oil, cinnamon, and salt.
3. Spread the almonds on the baking sheet and bake for 25 minutes.
4. Cool completely then store in an airtight container.

Nutrition: 170 calories, 15.5g fat, 5g protein, 5.5g carbs, 3.5g fiber, 2g net carbs

Baked Sesame Chia Crackers

Servings: 4

Ingredients:

- ¾ cup almond flour
- ¼ cup sesame seeds
- 1 tablespoon chia seeds
- ¼ teaspoon salt
- 2 teaspoons coconut oil, melted
- 1 large egg white

Instructions:

1. Preheat the oven to 350°F and line a baking sheet with parchment.
2. Whisk together the almond flour, sesame seeds, chia seeds, and salt.
3. Add the coconut oil and egg, stirring it into a soft dough.

4. Roll the dough out to 1/8-inch thick then cut it into squares.
5. Arrange the squares on the baking sheet and bake for 10 to 12 minutes until browned.

Nutrition: 200 calories, 18g fat, 7.5g protein, 7g carbs, 4g fiber, 3g net carbs

Coconut Chia Pudding

Servings: 3

Ingredients:

- 1 ¼ cup canned coconut milk
- 1 teaspoon vanilla extract
- ¼ teaspoon coconut extract
- Pinch salt
- Liquid stevia, to taste
- ¼ cup chia seeds

Instructions:

1. Whisk together the coconut milk, extracts, and salt in a bowl.
2. Sweeten with liquid stevia to taste then whisk in the chia seeds.
3. Cover and chill overnight then spoon into bowls to serve.

Nutrition: 315 calories, 30g fat, 6.5g protein, 12.5g carbs, 9g fiber, 3.5g net carbs

Baked Kale Chips

Servings: 4

Ingredients:

- 1 bunch fresh kale
- 1 tablespoon olive oil
- Salt and pepper

Instructions:

1. Preheat the oven to 350°F and line a baking sheet with foil.
2. Cut the kale into 2-inch pieces, removing the tough stems.
3. Toss with olive oil, salt, and pepper then spread on the baking sheet.
4. Bake for 10 to 12 minutes until crisp.

Nutrition: 50 calories, 3.5g fat, 1.5g protein, 4.5g carbs, 0.5g fiber, 4g net carbs

Chapter 7 3-Week Keto Diet Meal Plan for Beginners

The ketogenic diet is an excellent way to lose weight. While you do not necessarily need to count calories, you do need to stay within the recommended macronutrient ratio in order to enter and maintain a state of ketosis.

Luckily for you, this is easy with the help of three weekly meal plans!

All you have to do is follow the meal plans below. Each day you'll be enjoying quick and easy keto meals for breakfast, lunch, and dinner along with tasty snacks and smoothies. Feel free to enjoy these snacks and smoothies between meals or for dessert – you can customize the meal plan to suit your preferences!

Each recipe used in these meal plans features 6 or fewer main ingredients – that makes them incredibly easy to prepare and it won't bust your grocery budget! Do your best to follow the meal plans because they are designed to keep you within your macronutrient range, so you can maximize your benefits with the ketogenic diet. If you need an additional snack, make sure it is a healthy fat-heavy snack like sliced avocado or sugar-free full-fat Greek yogurt.

So, take a quick look at these meal plans then look for the recipes in the next chapter and weekly shopping lists in the back of the book. Good luck!

		Week 1 Meal Plan (Days 1 – 7)			
Day	**Breakfast**	**Lunch**	**Dinner**	**Snacks**	**Macros***
1	Ham and Cheddar Omelet with 3 Oz. Deli Ham	Balsamic Spinach Salad with Avocado	Broccoli Salmon Casserole	Almond Green Smoothie	**Calories**: 1730 **Fat**: 130g **Protein**: 110g **Net Carbs**: 21.5g
2	Cream Cheese Pancakes with 4 Slices Bacon	Balsamic Spinach Salad with Avocado and 6 oz. Deli Ham	Leftover Broccoli Salmon Casserole	Chocolate Almond Fat Bomb	**Calories**: 1700 **Fat**: 133.5g **Protein**: 100.5g **Net Carbs**: 17g
3	Leftover Cream Cheese Pancakes with 1 Cup Avocado	Chopped Tuna Salad with 1 Cup Avocado	Steak and Pepper Kebabs	2 Servings Classic Deviled Eggs	**Calories**: 1665 **Fat**: 127g **Protein**: 101.5g **Net Carbs**: 17.5g
4	Fried Eggs in Bell Peppers with 6 Slices Bacon	Leftover Balsamic Spinach Salad with Avocado and 3 Oz. Deli Ham	Leftover Broccoli Salmon Casserole	Chocolate Almond Fat Bomb	**Calories**: 1635 **Fat**: 127g **Protein**: 100g **Net Carbs**: 18g
5	Leftover Cream Cheese Pancakes with 1 Cup Avocado	Leftover Chopped Salad with Tuna and 1 Cup Avocado	Seared Lamb Chops	Cocoa Avocado Smoothie	**Calories**: 1690 **Fat**: 127g **Protein**: 102g **Net Carbs**: 18.5g
6	Leftover Fried Eggs in Bell Peppers with 4 Slices Bacon	Mexican Chicken Soup	Leftover Steak and Pepper Kebabs	Chocolate Almond Fat Bomb and 1 Cup Avocado	**Calories**: 1775 **Fat**: 136.5g **Protein**: 104.5g **Net Carbs**: 20.5g

| 7 | Creamy Coconut Porridge and 6 Slices Bacon | Leftover Mexican Chicken Soup | Leftover Seared Lamb Chops | 2 Servings Classic Deviled Eggs | **Calories**: 1710 **Fat**: 132g **Protein**: 110g **Net Carbs**: 15g |

* The daily calorie range for this meal plan is 1,600 to 1,800 calories

Week 1 Shopping List

Eggs, Meat, and Seafood

- Bacon – 20 slices
- Beef, sirloin steak – 12 ounces
- Chicken, boneless thighs – ½ pound
- Eggs – 26 large
- Ham, deli – 12 ounces
- Ham, diced – ½ cup
- Lamb chops, bone-in – 4 chops
- Salmon, Alaskan – 3 (6-ounce) cans
- Tuna, canned in water – 2 (5-ounce) cans

Dairy Products

- Butter – 2 tablespoons
- Cheddar cheese, shredded – 1 ¾ cups
- Cream cheese – ½ (8-ounce) package
- Heavy cream – 1 cup plus 2 tablespoons
- Mayonnaise – ½ cup

Refrigerated and Frozen Foods

- Almond milk, unsweetened – 2 cups
- Yogurt, full-fat Greek, plain – ½ cup

Fresh Fruits and Vegetables

- Avocado – 1 small, 6 medium
- Beans, green – 1 ½ cups
- Bell pepper, red – 2 small, 1 medium
- Broccoli – 1 pound
- Celery – 1 small stalk
- Cucumber, seedless – 1 small
- Garlic – 1 head
- Lemon – 2
- Onion, red – 1 small
- Onion, yellow – 1 small
- Romaine lettuce – 3 cups
- Spinach – 6 cups
- Tomatoes – 1 medium
- Tomatoes, cherry – ½ cup

Dried Goods and Pantry Staples

- Almonds – 8 whole
- Almond butter – ½ cup plus ½ tablespoon
- Almond flour – ½ cup
- Balsamic vinegar
- Broth, chicken – 1 cup
- Cocoa powder, unsweetened

- Coconut flour – 3 tablespoons
- Coconut milk, canned – ¼ cup
- Coconut oil
- Dijon mustard
- Ground psyllium husk
- Liquid stevia extract
- Olive oil
- Paprika
- Pepper
- Salt
- Whey protein powder, chocolate – 1 scoop

Week 2 Meal Plan (Days 8 - 14)				
Day	**Breakfast**	**Lunch**	**Dinner**	**Snacks**	**Macros***
8	Bacon Egg Cups with 1 Cup Avocado	Cheesy Cauliflower Soup	Smothered Pork Chops	Almond Butter Protein Shake and Cinnamon Spiced Almonds	**Calories**: 1780 **Fat**: 135.5g **Protein**: 110g **Net Carbs**: 20g
9	Leftover Bacon Egg Cups with 4 Slices Bacon	Bacon Arugula Salad with Mushrooms and Avocado Spinach Smoothie	Herb-Roasted Chicken	Pumpkin Pie Protein Shake	**Calories**: 1710 **Fat**: 126g **Protein**: 116.5g **Net Carbs**: 20g
10	Denver-Style Omelet	Leftover Cheesy Cauliflower Soup	Leftover Herb-Roasted Chicken	Baked Sesame Chia Crackers and Cocoa Almond Smoothie	**Calories**: 1665 **Fat**: 125.5g **Protein**: 108g **Net Carbs**: 22.5g
11	Eggs Baked in Avocado Boats with 4 Slices Bacon	Leftover Cheesy Cauliflower Soup with 6 Slices Bacon	Leftover Smothered Pork Chops	Baked Sesame Chia Crackers and Almond Green Smoothie	**Calories**: 1680 **Fat**: 127.5g **Protein**: 106.5g **Net Carbs**: 22g
12	Leftover Eggs Baked in Avocado Boats with 2 Slices Bacon	Leftover Bacon Arugula Salad with Mushrooms and 4 Slices Bacon	Cheese-Stuffed Burgers	Lemon Avocado Smoothie and Macadamia Nut Fat Bomb	**Calories**: 1690 **Fat**: 128.5g **Protein**: 108.5g **Net Carbs**: 15.5g
13	Three Cheese Omelet	Greek-Style Salad with Feta and 6 Ounces Deli Ham	Leftover Herb-Roasted Chicken	Macadamia Nut Fat Bomb	**Calories**: 1710 **Fat**: 130g **Protein**: 104.5g **Net Carbs**: 16g

| 14 | Spinach Breakfast Bowl with 4 Slices Bacon | Leftover Greek-Style Salad with Feta | Leftover Cheese-Stuffed Burgers | Strawberry Cheesecake Smoothie and Macadamia Nut Fat Bomb | **Calories**: 1690 **Fat**: 129g **Protein**: 112g **Net Carbs**: 16.5g |

* The daily calorie range for this meal plan is 1,600 to 1,800 calories

Week 2 Shopping List

Eggs, Meat, and Seafood

- Bacon – 41 slices
- Beef, ground (80% lean) – 12 ounces
- Chicken, bone-in thighs – 8 thighs
- Eggs – 22 large
- Ham, deli – 6 ounces
- Ham, diced – ¼ cup
- Pork, boneless loin chops – 12 ounces

Dairy Products

- Butter – 1 tablespoon
- Cheddar cheese, shredded – 2 ¾ cups
- Cream cheese – 2 tablespoons
- Feta cheese, crumbled – 1.5 ounces
- Heavy cream – 1 ¼ cups
- Parmesan cheese, grated – 2 tablespoons
- Sour cream – ¼ cup
- Swiss cheese, shredded – 2 tablespoons

Refrigerated and Frozen Foods

- Almond milk, unsweetened – 6 cups
- Yogurt, full-fat Greek, plain – ½ cup

Fresh Fruits and Vegetables

- Arugula, baby – 4 cups
- Avocado – 4 medium
- Beans, green – 1 ½ cups
- Bell pepper, green – 1 small
- Cauliflower – 2 small heads
- Celery – 2 small stalks
- Chives – 1 bunch
- Cucumber, seedless – 1 small
- Garlic – 1 head
- Lemon – 1
- Lettuce, Boston – 1 head
- Lettuce, romaine – 3 cups
- Mushrooms – 3 cups
- Onion, yellow – 1 small
- Raspberries – ¼ cup
- Shallot – 1 small
- Spinach – 6 cups

Dried Goods and Pantry Staples

- Almonds – 1 cup
- Almond butter – ½ cup plus 1 tablespoon
- Almond flour – 1 cup

- Broth, chicken – 2 ½ cups
- Chia seeds – 1 tablespoon
- Cocoa powder, unsweetened
- Coconut flour – 2 tablespoons
- Coconut milk, canned – ½ cup
- Coconut oil
- Dried herbs
- Garlic powder
- Ground cinnamon
- Kalamata olives – ½ cup
- Liquid stevia extract
- Macadamia nuts – 8 whole
- Onion powder
- Olive oil
- Pepper
- Pumpkin pie spice
- Pumpkin puree – 2 tablespoons
- Red wine vinegar
- Salt
- Sesame seeds – ¼ cup
- Vanilla extract
- Whey protein powder, chocolate – 1 scoop
- Whey protein powder, vanilla – 3 scoops

		Week 3 Meal Plan (Days 15 - 21)			
Day	Breakfast	Lunch	Dinner	Snacks	Macros*
15	One Pan Eggs and Peppers with 6 Ounces Deli Ham	Cucumber Avocado Soup with 6 Slices Bacon	Grilled Pesto Salmon	Vanilla Chai Smoothie and Sesame Seed Fat Bomb	**Calories**: 1770 **Fat**: 132.5g **Protein**: 110.5g **Net Carbs**: 22g
16	Leftover One Pan Eggs and Peppers with 1 Cup Avocado	Spinach Salad with Bacon Dressing and 4 Slices Bacon	Leftover Grilled Pesto Salmon	Lemon Avocado Smoothie and Sesame Seed Fat Bomb	**Calories**: 1765 **Fat**: 130.5g **Protein**: 112.5g **Net Carbs**: 24.5g
17	Chocolate Protein Pancakes with 2 Slices Bacon	Leftover Cucumber Avocado Soup with 6 Slices Bacon	Rosemary Pork Tenderloin	Cocoa Almond Smoothie with Sesame Seed Fat Bomb	**Calories**: 1760 **Fat**: 136g **Protein**: 114.5g **Net Carbs**: 21.5g
18	Leftover One Pan Eggs and Peppers with 6 Slices Bacon	Leftover Cucumber Avocado Soup with 4 Ounces Deli Ham	Curry Chicken and Broccoli	Pumpkin Pie Protein Shake and Sesame Seed Fat Bomb	**Calories**: 1770 **Fat**: 132g **Protein**: 116g **Net Carbs**: 21.5g
19	Leftover One Pan Eggs and Peppers with 6 Slices Bacon	Leftover Spinach Salad with Bacon Dressing and 1 Cup Avocado	Leftover Rosemary Pork Tenderloin	Sesame Seed Fat Bomb and 2 Ounces Deli Ham	**Calories**: 1750 **Fat**: 133.5g **Protein**: 105.5g **Net Carbs**:23.5g
20	Leftover Chocolate Protein Pancakes	Chopped Cobb Salad with Avocado and 3 Oz. Deli Ham	Leftover Curry Chicken and Broccoli	Coconut Chia Pudding	**Calories**: 1735 **Fat**: 134g **Protein**: 103g **Net Carbs**: 21g

21	Bacon Cheddar Chive Omelet	Leftover Chopped Cobb Salad with ½ Cup Avocado	Leftover Rosemary Pork Tenderloin	Raspberry Coconut Smoothie and 4 Slices Bacon	**Calories**: 1705 **Fat**: 125.5g **Protein**: 110.5g **Net Carbs**: 23.5g

* The daily calorie range for this meal plan is 1,600 to 1,800 calories

Week 3 Shopping List

Eggs, Meat, and Seafood

- Bacon – 40 slices
- Chicken breast, cooked – 1 cup
- Chicken thighs, boneless – 1 ½ pounds
- Eggs – 21 large
- Ham, deli – 17 ounces
- Pork tenderloin, boneless – 1 ¼ pounds
- Salmon, boneless – 2 (6-ounce) fillets

Dairy Products

- Butter – 1 tablespoon
- Blue cheese crumbles – 1 ounce
- Cheddar cheese, shredded – ¼ cup
- Heavy cream – ¼ cup

Refrigerated and Frozen Foods

- Almond milk, unsweetened – 4 cups

Fresh Fruits and Vegetables

- Asparagus – 16 spears
- Avocado – 2 small, 2 medium
- Bell pepper, green – 1 small
- Bell pepper, red – 1 small
- Broccoli – 5 cups
- Celery – 1 small stalk
- Chives – 1 bunch
- Cilantro – 1 bunch
- Cucumber, seedless – 1 medium
- Garlic – 1 head
- Lemon – 2
- Raspberries – 4 whole
- Romaine lettuce – 4 cups
- Rosemary – 1 bunch
- Spinach – 5 cups
- Tomatoes, cherry – ½ cup

Dried Goods and Pantry Staples

- Almond butter – ½ cup
- Almond flour – 2 tablespoons
- Apple cider vinegar
- Chia seeds – ¼ cup
- Cocoa powder, unsweetened
- Coconut extract
- Coconut milk, canned – 3 cups
- Coconut oil

- Curry powder
- Dijon mustard
- Garlic powder
- Ground cinnamon
- Ground cloves
- Ground cumin
- Ground ginger
- Honey
- Liquid stevia extract
- Olive oil
- Pepper
- Pesto – 2 tablespoons
- Pumpkin pie spice
- Pumpkin puree – 2 tablespoons
- Salt
- Sesame seeds, toasted – ¼ cup
- Vanilla extract
- Whey protein powder, chocolate – 1 scoop
- Whey protein powder, vanilla – 2 scoops

Conclusion

Grass-fed meat seared in high-quality butter, Greek yogurt topped with sweet berries, and vegetables cooked with bacon: these are all foods you are allowed on the ketogenic diet. While the keto diet is considered "restrictive" because it cuts out ingredients like grain, you'll soon discover that you can still eat really delicious meals. That's important because in many ways, the ketogenic diet is not easy. It's one of the most popular diets in America, however, and that's because of the benefits. Many find it easier to lose weight, they have more energy, and they don't have to worry about feeling hungry.

In this book, you learned what you have to do to get those benefits, and what exactly happens in the body during ketosis. The key is cutting out most carbs, especially simple ones that don't offer much nutrition, and replacing those calories with fat. The body learns to adjust to fat as its main source of fuel and starts producing ketones. All the food you eat needs to have limited carbs and lots of fat, or else the balance tips and the body leaves ketosis.

This book provided a thorough checklist of foods and brands you can eat on the keto diet. It also gave some tips on how to eat out and travel while the keto diet, since those are times when it can be hard to stick to a strict eating routine. By doing menu research beforehand, packing keto-friendly snacks, and giving yourself a little room to breathe, you can stay faithful to the keto lifestyle *and* enjoy yourself.

The ketogenic diet isn't for everybody and there are potentially serious risks associated with it. By educating yourself, planning meals ahead of time, and watching your electrolytes, you can ensure your success and best health. Talk to your doctor before going on the keto diet and surround yourself with positive, helpful support. You can enjoy the best health of your life by switching your eating habits. Consider switching to the ketogenic diet.

Printed in Great
Britain
by Amazon